THE PETER WITT STREETCARS OF CLEVELAND

James A. Toman   •   James R. Spangler

PUBLISHING INFORMATION

Published by
Cleveland Landmarks Press, Inc.
13610 Shaker Boulevard, Suite 503
Cleveland, Ohio 44120-1592
www.clevelandlandmarkspress.com
(216) 658 4144

ISBN: 978-0-936760-31-5

LIBRARY OF CONGRESS CONTROL NUMBER
2011913514

Designed by
John Yasenosky, III

Printed by
Sheridan Books, Inc.
Chelsea, Michigan

Inside Front Cover

Top: Cleveland Transit System (CTS) 260, a streetcar from the original Peter Witt fleet makes its way down the center reservation of Brookpark Road in 1949. The car is on a fan trip, and the destination sign is part of the fan high jinks. *(Northern Ohio Railway Museum Collection, Russ Schram photo)*

Center: Cleveland Transit System 168 is maneuvering through the Brooklyn Car House yard in 1951. *(Jim Buckley photo)*

Bottom: An April 27, 1952, "Parade of Progress" marked the end of streetcar service on Cleveland's main street, Euclid Avenue. Car 0363, a work car converted from the 450 series of Peter Witts, represented the fleet. *(Jim Spangler collection)*

Inside Back Cover

Top: Nearing the southern end of the East 55th Street line at War Loop, CTS 1304 rambles along still-brick-paved East 71st Street in 1951. *(Jim Buckley photo)*

Center: Articulated CTS 5022 glides along a short stretch of center reservation track on Euclid Avenue in Cleveland's University Circle neighborhood in 1951. *(Jim Spangler collection)*

Bottom: Turning from State Road onto Brookpark Road, CTS 4078 is headed for the end-of-the-line loop only a short distance away. *(Bill Vigrass photo)*

INTRODUCTION

The inventive spirit of Cleveland and the Western Reserve has been well documented. Many know of Clevelander Charles Brush, his invention of the arc light, and his giving to Cleveland's Public Square the world's first outdoor lighting. They probably have heard that Cleveland had the first electric streetcar line, built by Edward Bentley and Walter Knight on Central Avenue (although their method of electrification was soon eclipsed by developments in Richmond, Virginia). Many also know that Cleveland was the first city to have a municipal airport, which featured the first air traffic control tower and the first provision for lighting the runways for night-time flying. Later it became the first airport connected to its downtown by a rail rapid transit line.

Cleveland was the nation's early leader in the development of the automobile. Alexander Winton's automobile factory on Berea Road was the largest in the world. Cleveland ingenuity produced the steering wheel, the sealed headlight beam, and the diesel engine. The city was also the first to establish an automobile club, Cleveland's chapter today being the oldest in the American Automobile Association consortium.

While Cleveland's leading role in transportation innovation is generally acknowledged, except for the traction enthusiast, relatively few are aware of the transforming influence Cleveland creativity had on the street railway industry, both throughout the United States as well as internationally.

From Cleveland came the Car Rider's Car, featuring a pay-as-you-pass fare collection procedure. Designed by Cleveland political activist and city traction commissioner Peter Witt, and ever after better known by his name rather than by its formal title, the Car Rider's Car greatly improved street railway efficiency in Cleveland. Its success in its home city prompted other cities across the country and overseas to adopt the design as an effective way of responding to steady increases in ridership and to the complications posed by worsening urban traffic.

Cleveland's streetcar era came to an end in 1954. But elsewhere Peter Witts continued in service. The resilience of the model is well attested by the role the Witts continue to play on San Francisco's historic F line. There a fleet of second-hand Peter Witts, purchased from Milan, Italy, join with more modern PCC cars in providing dependable service on the heavily patronized line.

Almost 100 years from its first appearance in Cleveland, the Peter Witt car is still soldiering on.

Ex-Milan, Italy, Peter Witts share service with PCC cars on San Francisco's historic F line. In 2003, car1848 covers the Market Street right-of-way as it heads for the Castro. (*Jim Toman photo*)

A NEW ERA BEGINS

For the Cleveland transit patron, March 1910 came in like a lamb, ending two long winters of streetcar strife that had disrupted service and made travel schedules unreliable.

The battle for control of the city transit lines had begun in earnest in 1902 when an ally of Cleveland Mayor Tom L. Johnson had been granted a franchise to operate streetcars along Fulton Road. The line would charge a three-cent fare.

The development set off financial alarms in the headquarters of the chief Cleveland traction operators, the Cleveland City Railway and the Cleveland Electric Railway, who then were charging five cents a ride on their lines. The two companies' response was to merge, under the latter name, and to use the courts to try to block any further expansion of the Johnson interests.

The struggle went back and forth, but eventually Johnson's Municipal Traction Company (MTC) seemed to triumph. On April 27, 1908, it took control of the city's streetcar services. Municipal Traction Company's victory proved ephemeral. Service interruptions, a transit workers' strike, and even some violence marred the apparent triumph, and eventually these led to MTC's bankruptcy.

From the time of the Tayler Grant to his untimely demise in 1926, John Stanley brought to the Cleveland Railway Company (CRC) presidency great vision and managerial skill.
(Cleveland State University Michael Schwartz Library, Cleveland Press Collection)

On November 13, 1908, the messy situation ended up in the courtroom of U. S. Judge Robert W. Taylor. After some 15 months of deliberation, Taylor announced his proposed solution (which came to be known as the Taylor Grant). It gave the Cleveland Railway Company (CRC) (the "Electric" had been dropped from its name) ownership of the traction properties and a guarantee of a six-percent annual return on its investment. The city was granted the right to set service standards; its interests would be monitored by a traction commissioner appointed by the mayor. Fares were to be based on the cost of the service. If any conflict arose over the terms of the agreement, it would be settled by arbitration.

The City Council of Cleveland crafted an ordinance embracing these terms which granted Cleveland Railway Company a 25-year franchise to operate on the streets of the city. The citizens went to the polls on February 17, 1910, and gave their consent to the ordinance. The trustees of the Railway, led by its president, John J. Stanley, followed suit and approved the terms of the franchise. The last roadblock out of the way, the Cleveland Railway Company era began on March 1, 1910.

Public Square is relatively quiet on a Sunday morning in 1911. Two pre-Witt streetcars make their downtown loop, from Superior Avenue onto Ontario Street. *(Cleveland State University Michael Schwartz Library, Bruce Young Collection)*

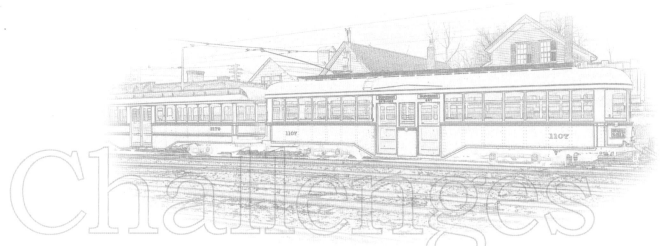

CLEVELAND RAILWAY TACKLES ITS CHALLENGES

The ordinance which governed the relationship between the City and Cleveland Railway Company imposed a demand for improvements in the Railway's fleet of streetcars.

Upon the start of its operational control, CRC had 950 streetcars which had come from the predecessor companies. In a letter to Cleveland Mayor Herman C. Baehr, CRC President John J. Stanley acknowledged, "There is immediate necessity for additional cars... we are willing and anxious to add to our equipment." Ridership was rapidly increasing. During Cleveland Railway's first year of control, passenger tallies had climbed 18.5 percent to 228.2 million. Stanley asserted that CRC "ought to have now 200 new cars."

The company's first major effort to address the need for these new cars came in the form of an order for 53 new models from Cleveland-based G. C. Kuhlman Car Company. The cars, numbered 1000-1052, entered service in 1913. Passengers paid their fares as they entered via a rear door. They exited from the front door.

At about the same time, CRC placed another, larger order with Kuhlman for 201 more cars. These cars featured double center doors, separated by a conductor's station. The fleet carried the numbers 1100-1300, but these streetcars were generally known as the "1200s." They arrived on the CRC property between late 1913 and early 1915.

In 1911, a single automobile makes its way through Public Square. Six Cleveland Railway pre-Peter Witt streetcars and three horse-drawn carriages share the roadways. *(Cleveland State University Michael Schwartz Library, Bruce Young Collection)*

By 1923, automobile traffic through Public Square has increased significantly. The view looks east, across the ponds on the Square's southwest quadrant. *(Cleveland State University Michael Schwartz Library, Bruce Young Collection)*

In 1929 Cleveland Railway 1011 enters the Euclid Beach loop, the eastern terminus for one of the St. Clair Avenue
car line branches. The front-entrance, rear-exit 1000 series streetcars were an early effort to upgrade the Cleveland fleet.
(Cleveland State University Michael Schwartz Library, Gerald E. Brookins Collection, Harry Christiansen photo)

Cleveland Railway 1004, hauling trailer 2359, pauses on Superior Avenue at East 105th Street.
(Cleveland State University Michael Schwartz Library, Bruce Young Collection)

The center-entrance/exit 1200 fleet entered service in 1914-1915. Unit 1245 is heading for downtown Cleveland on the Clifton Boulevard line. *(Jim Spangler collection)*

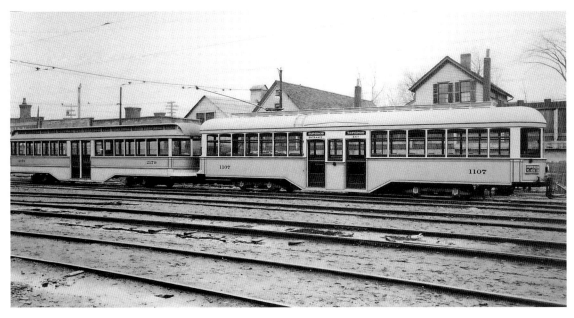

A trailer is hooked up to center-entrance car 1107 at Superior Station.
Trailer operation was a significant part of Cleveland Railway operations.
(Cleveland State University Michael Schwartz Library, Gerald E. Brookins Collection, Harry Christiansen photo)

PETER WITT BECOMES CITY RAILROAD COMMISSIONER

Peter Witt was a political activist and a close associate of the progressive Cleveland Mayor Tom L. Johnson, and had served as city clerk during the Johnson administration (1901-1909). Johnson was replaced as mayor by Herman Baehr in the 1909 election, and it was during Baehr's short term in office that the Taylor Grant went into effect. Baehr named Gerhard Dahl as the city's first street railroad commissioner.

When Democrat Newton D. Baker, the city's law director under Tom L. Johnson, was elected Cleveland mayor in 1912, he appointed his friend and former colleague Peter Witt to be the city's second transit commissioner, replacing Gerhard Dahl. That role gave Witt the platform to bring about improvements to streetcar service.

With headway between cars as close as it could come, Witt introduced to Cleveland City Council an ordinance requiring Cleveland Railway to invest in 100 non-motorized trailer cars. It was not a decision that the Railway's executives favored,

but John Stanley acknowledged the city's right to control the nature of the streetcar service, "including the right to determine the character of the cars."

Stanley pointed out that while using trailer cars doubled capacity, their added weight also resulted in slower operating speed. Consequently in the Company's judgment, they did not represent the ideal solution for improving service. Nonetheless, Cleveland Railway decided to purchase 300 trailers (fleet number 2000-2299) from the Kuhlman Car Company. The new trailers were in service by 1913, but while the trailers added seating capacity, the system still was having difficulty in achieving scheduled speeds.

Witt recognized that the key factor in preventing the streetcars from meeting schedule requirements was the amount of time they lost while passengers boarded or exited. If a streetcar design could result in faster passenger boarding and exiting, scheduled speed could be more nearly accomplished. Pondering a solution to this problem led to Witt designing a new style streetcar, one which would operate on a pay-as-you-pass fare-collecting system, instead of the traditional pay-as-you-enter or pay-as-you-leave systems then in place. The idea was really simple, but at the same time it was also ingenious.

Witt designed a streetcar with wide front and center doors. Boarding passengers would enter at the front, but they would not pay fares at this point. The front half of the car featured longitudinal seating, which also allowed for more standee space. The conductor was stationed at the center door. If a passenger wanted to sit in the rear of the car, fitted with more appealing transverse seating, he or she would deposit their fare as they passed the conductor station. Passengers remaining in the front of the car would pay their fares when exiting at the center door. This system resulted in roughly half the riders exiting at any one time being pre-paid. The conductor's job was trimmed to service only the passengers exiting from the front half of the car. This overall arrangement speeded both entering and exiting.

Witt asked the shop force at Cleveland Railway's Lakeview Shops (East 118th Street and Euclid Avenue) to manufacture the car. Officially named the Car Rider's Car, but informally nicknamed "Pete's Pet," the first model, numbered as car 33, was turned over to Cleveland Railway on December 1, 1914. The model received its patent April 25, 1916.

This pre-production model easily garnered plaudits from the CRC officials, who went on to place an order with the G. C. Kuhlman Company of Cleveland for a fleet of 130 more.

Over the years, Cleveland Railway would go on to purchase or to produce itself a total of seven fleets of "Peter Witt" cars. Though the Cleveland Transit System, which took over ownership of the city's transportation network in 1942, would briefly (1946-1952) operate a small fleet of Presidents' Conference Committee (PCC) streamliners, the Peter Witt fleets continued to carry the large majority of the system's riders.

The last day for streetcars in Cleveland came on January 24, 1954. The very last car to run was Peter Witt 4142.

A plaque, identifying the car model as a Car Rider's Car, and stipulating its approval for a U. S. patent, appeared in every Peter Witt streetcar. (*Jim Toman collection*)

Progressive political figure Peter Witt served as Cleveland's street railway commissioner from 1911-1915. In that post he invented the Car Rider's Car. The success of his design resulted in Witt's name ever being associated with the front-entrance, center-exit streetcar. Witt later served as a Cleveland councilman, and ran (unsuccessfully) for both Cleveland mayor and Ohio governor. *(Cleveland State University Michael Schwartz Library, Cleveland Press Collection)*

The first Peter Witt streetcar rests in a Cleveland Railway car yard. It is "showing its stuff" in test runs along West 65th Street. Test results were so positive that the design became the mainstay of Cleveland street railway operations and was widely adopted across the country and beyond. *(Jim Spangler collection)*

The interior of car 33 shows the Peter Witt seating arrangement. The longitudinal seating at the front of the car is
for passengers who have not yet paid their fares. The transverse seating, past the conductor's station, is for paid riders.
(Jim Spangler collection)

This view of car 241 illustrates the seating arrangement from the rear towards the operator's compartment.
(Jim Spangler collection)

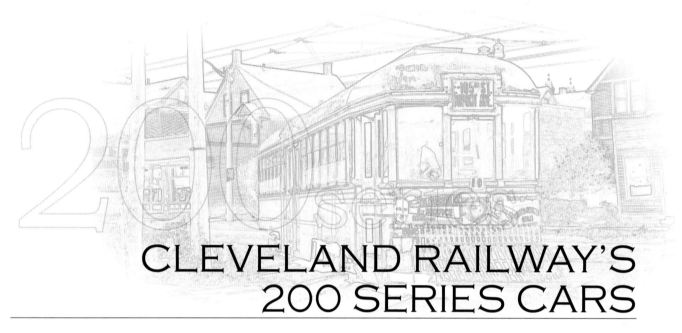

CLEVELAND RAILWAY'S 200 SERIES CARS

Having monitored Witt's car 33 in trial operation, Railway officials were convinced the company should proceed with acquiring a fleet designed according to the Peter Witt prototype. The company turned to its favorite builder, Cleveland's G. C. Kuhlman Company, with its order (in fact, all future Cleveland Railway orders would be placed with Kuhlman). The order was divided into two parts. The first part was for cars numbered 200-249, and the second for cars 250-329. (The original car, Witt's 33, was renumbered as 330.) The first 50 cars were delivered in 1915, the remainder in 1916. The cars were officially identified on the Railway roster as Type 23, but commonly known as the 200s.

The 200s were 51 feet in length, with wide double-sized doors at front and center. The cars seated 55. The conductor's station was located just front of the center doors. A coal stove was located at the front of the car, immediately behind the motorman's station. The arch roof sported a clerestory designed by shop mechanic Terrance Scullin. At the front of the car was an Eclipse fender (more commonly called a "cow-catcher").

The 200s had a long service life. Units from the fleet were retired between 1947 and 1951. Scrapping at the Harvard Shops came soon after retirement.

From the East 55th Operating Station on Harvard Avenue, Cleveland Railway 299 is ready to enter service, heading for the northern end of the crosstown East 55th Street line. *(Cleveland Railway Company, Doc Rollins photo)*

Cleveland Railway 307 pulls matching trailer 2343 at the Hough operating station at East 105th Street. *(Cleveland State University Michael Schwartz Library, Bruce Young Collection)*

Car 249, in the original Cleveland Railway yellow and cream livery, is at the busy Woodhill operating station, which served seven east side streetcar lines. *(Cleveland State University Michael Schwartz library, Bruce Young Collection)*

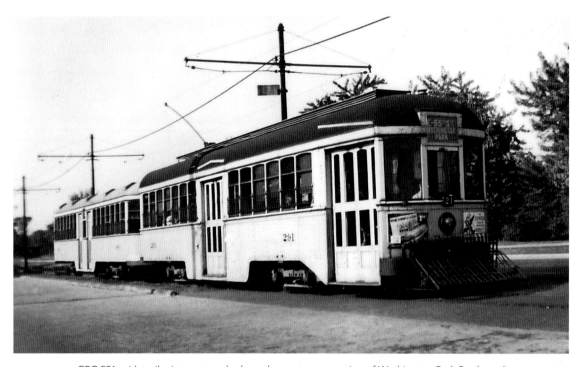

CRC 291, with trailer in tow, travels along the center reservation of Washington Park Boulevard
on its way to the line's end at Harvard and East 49th Street.
(Cleveland State University Michael Schwartz Library, Gerald E. Brookins Collection, Harry Christiansen photo)

In 1940, Peter Witt 229, modeling its stylish Raymond Loewy livery in green, grey, and white colors, is on layover at the end of the Buckeye Road line at East 130th Street. *(Jim Spangler collection)*

Cleveland Transit System 237, showing its age, pulls into Aetna Loop, making a short turn on the long East 105th Street line. The destination sign shows that the car will turn back north, heading for Dupont Loop. It is in the lighter version of the Loewy paint scheme, which remained the fleet colors until the end of rail operations. *(Bill Vigrass photo)*

On a short-turn run to Cedar Glen, a 200-series Witt, sporting a modified fender, makes its way east on Euclid Avenue.
(Cleveland State University Michael Schwartz Library, Bruce Young Collection)

CTS 254 has just activated the switch for a right turn onto Denison Avenue. It is heading for the Denison operation station at West 73rd Street. *(Bill Vigrass photo)*

CTS 310 rattles across the intersection of East 93rd Street and Union Avenue. It is on its way to the Garfield Park loop. *(Bill Vigrass photo)*

CLEVELAND RAILWAY'S 450 & 400 SERIES CARS

After Cleveland Railway had enjoyed eight consecutive years of passenger increases, in 1918, America's first full year engaged in World War I, the Company saw passenger tallies drop by 23 million rides. By 1920, however, that loss was more than made up, as ridership in the next two years increased by 75 million, to almost 451 million. In the same stretch of time, the Railway had retired 85 of its oldest streetcars. The need for additions to the streetcar fleet was apparent.

In February 1920, Cleveland Railway placed an order with the G.C. Kuhlman Company for 50 Peter Witt model motor cars and for another 50 trailers (2451-2500) of matching design. This motor fleet was identified as Cleveland Railway Type 26 and carried fleet numbers 450-499.

The 450s had several features different from the 200s. The most immediately apparent was that the front destination sign was placed at the side rather than at the center.

Also readily apparent was the configuration for the sliding center doors. They were split, with the conductor's platform between them, rather than in front of them as had been the case with the 200s. Less obvious was the change to the front entry door, which was one foot wider than in the 200s. Experience had shown that the 44-inch width of the front door on the earlier Peter Witt fleet had caused boarding passengers to jostle one another, resulting in slower entry. Gone from the roof was the Scullin ventilator, replaced by 10 separate units, five to each side of the roof.

The 450s entered service in the second half of 1920, together with their matching trailers plying the busy Euclid Avenue line. The bulk of the fleet remained in service until retirement in 1948 and 1949. Cars from this fleet were scrapped at Harvard Shops by the end of 1951.

Ridership dipped by more than 11 percent in 1921, but despite this loss Cleveland Railway President John

Stanley stated that the Company needed to be ready for the time when it would carry 500 million passengers annually (a prediction that never came to fruition). To prepare for this increased service demand, CR once again turned to G. C. Kuhlman Company with another order for both motor cars and trailers.

Arriving during the second half of 1923 were 100 Peter Witt cars, 350-449, Cleveland Railway Type 25 (except for car 350, Type 24, which had General Electric motors while the remainder of the fleet were Westinghouse powered). Arriving at about the same time were 50 center-entrance trailers, number 2376-2825.

The motor fleet, typically referred to as the 400s, looked just like the earlier 450s, with the wider front door and split center-exit doors, and the arch roof with 10 ventilators. There were some mechanical differences from the earlier model. The 400s had a built-in bottom front step versus the drop style on the 450s, and they featured mechanically operated folding doors at the center. At a glance, however, the two fleets appeared identical. The 400s, often pulling trailers, operated on many lines, both east side and west side.

The first of these units were withdrawn from service in 1948, and most were gone by April 8, 1951, when service on St. Clair Avenue beyond E 129th Street was turned over to buses. This date also marked the end of trailer operation on the St. Clair trunk line. A few of the 400 series survived a bit longer, on call out of Denison Station.

Seating in the 450 series was the same as in the original 200s. A conductor mans his station between the center doors, while a Cleveland police officer hitches a free ride to his beat.
(*Cleveland State University Michael Schwartz Library, Bruce Young Collection*)

A new Cleveland Railway 452 is parked in front of Windermere Station, and will soon depart for downtown Cleveland on the Euclid Avenue line. A conductor stands at his station between the sliding center doors. *(Jim Spangler collection)*

In this 1937 scene, St. Paul's Episcopal Church, at Fairmount and Coventry boulevards forms the backdrop for Cleveland Railway 461 which is heading for the Fairmount terminus at Canterbury Road. *(Stephen Maguire photo, Jim Toman collection)*

Less than a year old, Cleveland Railway 418 is parked in Brooklyn Station, which served Broadview, Pearl, and State streetcar lines on the city's southwest side. *(Malcolm McCarter photo, Jim Spangler collection)*

Cleveland Railway 401, with matching trailer 2383, pulls into Brooklyn Station.
(Cleveland State University Michael Schwartz Library, Gerald E. Brookins Collection, Harry Christiansen photo)

Pulling trailer 2389, in 1938 Cleveland Railway 427 passes through Public Square in downtown Cleveland. The car will pick up riders headed to the Cleveland Air Show at the airport. *(Stephen Maguire photo, Jim Toman collection)*

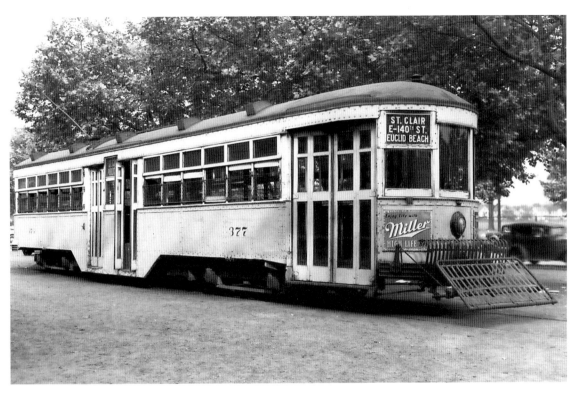

Car 377, from the 400 series, shows its differences from the 450 fleet. The center doors fold, and the front step is built in. It is in Euclid Beach Park loop. *(Jim Spangler collection)*

In the absence of a crowd, a passenger uses the center door to board car 385 in front of the Society for Savings Bank on Public Square. *(Cleveland State University Michael Schwartz Library, Bruce Young Collection)*

CRC 363 stops at Woodland Avenue and Woodhill Road. The Woodhill Homes subsidized housing project is under construction in the background. *(Cleveland State University Michael Schwartz Library, Gerald E. Brookins Collection, Harry Christiansen photo)*

Peter Witt 415 rests in Kamm's Corners, at the intersection of Lorain Avenue and Rocky River Drive. *(Cleveland State University Michael Schwartz Library, Gerald E. Brookins Collection, Harry Christiansen photo)*

CTS 416 speeds down the West 6th ramp to the Detroit-Superior Bridge subway.
The subway gave streetcars a speedy, private right-of-way to the west side of the city. *(Bill Vigrass photo)*

Hauling a trailer car, CTS 409 is inbound on the Broadview Road branch of the West 25th Street car line.
(Cleveland State University Michael Schwartz Library, Gerald E. Brookins Collection, Harry Christiansen photo)

Car 456 is parked in the Canterbury wye at the eastern end of the Fairmount car line. Its destination sign indicates that it is headed only to the Cedar Operating Station at East 109th Street. *(Bill Vigrass photo)*

The long East 105th Street car line had several short-turn loops or wyes. In 1945 car 367 rests in the Bancroft wye, the last cut-off before the Garfield Park loop. *(Lawrence Bochning photo, Jim Spangler collection)*

Returning from a trip to Cleveland Heights, CTS 455 arrives at Cedar Glen. The overpass served
New York Central and Cleveland Union Terminal trains. *(Bill Vigrass photo)*

The last of the 450s sit dejectedly in St. Clair Station. The crude paint on their sides "celebrated" their final run,
April 8, 1951; St. Clair Avenue streetcar service east of East 129th Street ended the previous day. *(Jim Spangler photo)*

CLEVELAND RAILWAY'S 100 SERIES PETER WITTS

In March 1924, Cleveland Railway faced a challenge from a newly formed company seeking a franchise to operate a motor coach system in the city. Cleveland Railway naturally opposed the franchise, and ultimately its opposition proved convincing to the city fathers. Nonetheless, CR President John Stanley was determined to stave off any future threats of competition. While he was not truly in favor of undertaking bus operation, he conceded that "If busses are needed in Cleveland, this company should operate them." He added, "we must operate them if the determination is made that they are to be run."

Thus pressured into the bus business, in 1925 Cleveland Railway purchased 30 single-deck motor coaches from a joint G.C. Kuhlmann/ White Motor partnership for 1925 delivery. It then went on to order a fleet of 59 double-deck buses from Safeway Six Wheel, the first 19 of which arrived in 1925. None of these buses were intended as replacements for streetcars, but rather to serve in supplemental or complementary roles.

At the same time Cleveland Railway had been continuing its practice of retiring streetcars inherited from its pre-1910 predecessors. The company scrapped 121 of the older cars during 1924 and 1925. These needed to be replaced.

The financial requirements of funding the bus purchases prompted CR to seek savings on this next fleet of streetcars. Rather than return to Kuhlman with another order, CR management determined it would be more cost effective to utilize its skilled crew of mechanics stationed at its expansive Harvard Shops to tackle the job. The first 25 of these cars were numbered 150-174 and catalogued as CR Type 27. The first of the new cars, originally numbered as 1301, came off the production line in September 1924. The remainder became available during the first quarter of 1925. The cars were originally assigned to service on the East 79th and Kinsman lines.

The 100s were modeled on the floor plan of the original 200 series Witts. The main difference was in their wider front door, but like the 200s, their center doors were together, with the conductor's platform to their front. The arch roof was also different; it followed the style adopted for the 400s and 450s. The 100s seated 56, the front half of the cars with longitudinal rattan seats; the rear half with transverse seating.

The new streetcars outlasted the new buses, and when the latter were scrapped, most of the 100s received the buses' leather seats.

In a subsequent rebuilding, the cars were converted for one-man operation and received new interior lighting and electric heat. The 100s continued in service until 1951. They were scrapped at Harvard in 1952.

The front end of CRC 151 was typical of the early Peter Witt fleets. A no-smoking sign, fixed above a Chesterfield advertisement, and a sign telling passengers that spitting was prohibited by city ordinance cover the rear of the motorman's cab. A Peter Smith coal stove is to the left. *(Jim Spangler collection)*

Fresh from the production line in 1925, CRC 156 poses in a snowy Harvard Yard. *(Jim Spangler collection)*

Cleveland Railway 154 rests in the Bessemer Loop at the southern end of the East 79th Street car line. The loop was on property the Railway had eyed as the site for a future operating station. *(Jim Spangler collection)*

In this post-World War II photo, car 152 has lost its conductor's station at the center door, as the 100s were converted to one-man operation. The car also shows off its more comfortable replacement leather seats.
(Cleveland State University Michael Schwartz Library, Gerald E. Brookins Collection)

The Baldwin Reservoir forms the backdrop for car 152 in the wye at the end of the Scovill Avenue line.
The Scovill streetcar line was the first line to be converted to buses following World War II. (Jim Spangler collection)

In its light-colored Loewy paint scheme, CTS 156 waits in the Brussels wye at the end of
the Nottingham branch of the St. Clair Avenue line. *(Jim Spangler collection)*

On March 18, 1950, CTS 166 crosses East 55th Street on the Kinsman Avenue line. In one week's time,
the line will be converted to trackless trolley operation. *(Anthony Krisak photo)*

CTS 159 turns from High Street onto East Fourth Street. It is on the Union Avenue line, headed for
East 130th Street and Corlett Avenue. *(Bill Vigrass photo)*

In April 1952, CTS car 172 travels along Lansing Avenue, just west of East 65th Street. *(Jim Spangler collection)*

CLEVELAND RAILWAY'S 1300 SERIES PETER WITTS

The 1300s were the second installment of the Cleveland Railway-built cars. Numbered 1300-1376, they arrived between April and November 1925.

The most noticeable difference in these cars from the 100s was their having the split center-exit folding doors, with the conductor's station between them. Cars 1300-1372 were designated Type 28. Type 29 was assigned to 1373-1375, which had leather (rather than rattan) seats and a different kind of ventilating system from the other cars.

Experimental car 1376, Type 30, however, was the unique member of the fleet. It was constructed entirely of aluminum, resulting in six tons lower weight than the other 1300s. During the 1926 American Electric Railway Association convention in Cleveland, 1376 was displayed on the stage of Public Hall. In operation, 1376 proved to be less than satisfactory. Its light weight resulted in sliding on wet rails, and it was too light to pull a trailer.

Like the 100s, later rebuilding of the 1300s resulted in leather seating, new interior lighting, and electric heat.

Following the end of World War II, the transit union agreed to the practice of instituting one-man operation of streetcars, and most of the 1300s were eventually converted to one-man cars. Not all, however, and the last two-man cars to run were 1300s on the Lorain Avenue line which ended streetcar service on June 14, 1952.

With the Lorain line's conversion to trackless trolley operation, the 1300s became surplus, and except for 1361, they were all scrapped at Harvard during 1952. It was 1361's fate to become the shop's Judas goat, towing other cars to the scrap line. Its turn with the torch came in 1954.

Pulling railroad-roof trailer 2103, CRC 1371 reaches Superior Avenue at East 105th Street.
(Cleveland Railway photo, Jim Spangler collection)

Not much in the way of luxury, before their conversion to one-man cars, there was no farebox at the front.
One sign touts sales of 50,000 weekly passes (at $1.25), and another reminds riders that motormen are not permitted
to carry on conversations with them. *(Jim Spangler collection)*

CRC 1375 was one of four cars in the series to be built with comfortable leather seating.
The other 72 units of the 1300 fleet came with rattan seats. *(Jim Spangler collection)*

When the Cleveland Indians played a home game at old League Park at Lexington Avenue and E. 66th Street,
streetcars would lay over awaiting the crush crowd at game's end. Here 1369 and trailer 2333 are ready for action.
(Cleveland State University Michael Schwartz Library, Gerald E. Brookins Collection, Harry Christiansen photo)

Having left the East Ninth Street Pier loop, CRC 1372 heads south. A Great Lakes passenger steamer can be seen in the background. During the summer boating season, the line was well patronized. *(Cleveland State University Michael Schwartz Library, Gerald E. Brookins Collection, Harry Christiansen photo)*

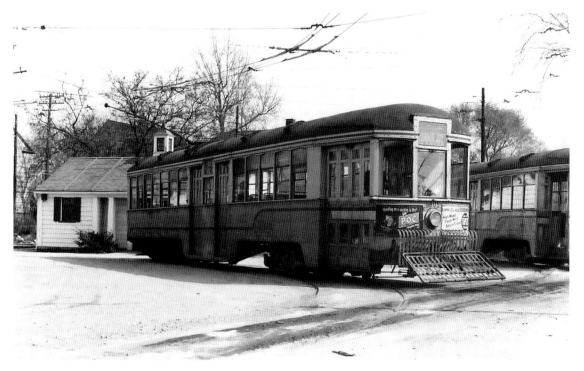

A few 1300s were never converted for one-man operation. Here two-man 1305 is leaving the West 140th Street loop of the Lorain Avenue car line   It is April 1952; there only two months left for streetcars on Lorain. *(Jim Spangler photo)*

CTS 1353 awaits passengers at the Taylor Road wye on the Cedar Avenue car line in May 1945. In a month, this outer portion of the Cedar line will give way to buses, with Cedar streetcars operating only to Cedar Glen. *(Anthony Krisak photo)*

In 1952, westbound CTS 1341 stops at the former Woodland Avenue and Westside Railroad station at West 98th Street and Lorain Avenue. *(Roy Bruce photo)*

The Fulton Road line was one of the system's more lightly patronized, but it served well patrons traveling to and from the Cleveland Zoo. Here CTS 1372 heads for Archwood loop. *(Bernard Polinak photo)*

The last streetcar line in Cleveland to operate with trailers was East 55th Street.   On the last day, June 16, 1951, car 1308 and trailer are ready to leave the line's northern terminus at Marquette Avenue.
(Cleveland State University Michael Schwartz Library, Gerald E. Brookins Collection, Harry Christiansen photo)

CLEVELAND RAILWAY'S ARTICULATED PETER WITTS

In 1927, Cleveland Railway took possession of its first articulated streetcar, one of a fleet of 28 to be built by the G. C. Kuhlman Car Company. Twenty-four more of the cars would arrive in 1928, and the last three in 1929.

The articulated cars, numbered 5000-5027 and identified at CR Type 31, were 101 feet in length and could seat 100 passengers, 44 in the front car, 56 in the rear car.

They weighed 80,400 pounds. Despite the weight, because the cars had six motors, the slowing problem encountered by a four-motor car pulling a trailer was eliminated. The 5000s were sleek in appearance. Their ventilators lay nearly flat against the arch roof, and a recessed Eclipse C fender added to the fleet's modern profile. Car 5000 was a featured display at the 1927 American Electric Railway Association convention in Cleveland. Following the convention, the first articulated went into regular service in October 1927.

Car 5000 originally carried split destination signs in front and on the side, and its front windows were all the same size. The Railway decided that it preferred a single destination board, and it asked for a wider center window panel at the front of the car. Car 5000 was renovated in this fashion, and all the other cars in the fleet were delivered with the revised styling.

Passengers were pleased by the amenities the new fleet offered. There were transverse leather seats throughout, overhead lighting was recessed under a frosted dome to reduce glare, and dependable electric heating provided even temperature throughout the cars.

Because of their length and required turning radius, the 5000s were assigned to only two routes, Euclid Avenue on the east side, operating from Windermere Station, and Detroit Avenue on the west side, operating from Rocky River Station. During World War II, the fleet operated exclusively as Euclid cars.

The Cleveland Transit System, which had taken control of the sytem in 1942, was committed to eliminating streetcar service in favor of either bus or trackless trolley operation. The post-war years saw the steady conversion of the streetcar routes. April 26, 1952, marked the final day for streetcars on Euclid Avemue, Cleveland's main street.

The next day, however, streetcars had a last hurrah on the avenue.

A throng of 300,000 Clevelanders lined Euclid Avenue to witness a transportation "Parade of Progress." Car 5025 represented the fleet of articulateds in that event. After the parade, it headed to retirement at the East 55th Station. Transit officials hoped that there might be some interested buyers for the 5000s, but none came forward. The cars were all scrapped at Harvard on March 24, 1953.

An articulation joint connected the front and rear cars, resulting in the unit sporting a 101-foot length. (Northern Ohio Railway Museum Collection)

In 1927, newly completed articulated car 5000 poses at the Kuhlman Car Company. *(Jim Spangler collection)*

In September 1927, Cleveland Railway officials take a test ride on a new articulated unit.
(Plain Dealer *photo, Jim Spangler collection)*

CTS 5002 shares Rocky River yard with other 5000s. These cars are stationed on the west side for
Detroit Avenue service. The rest of the 5000 fleet are at Windermere, for Euclid Avenue service.
(Cleveland State University Michael Schwartz Library, Gerald E. Brookins Collection)

In 1928, CRC 5005 pauses on Euclid Avenue at East 24th Street, as it heads east to Windermere Station.
(Jim Spangler collection)

Articulated unit 5010 passes the Fenn College campus in 1952 on its way east to Windermere Station. *(Jim Spangler photo)*

Articulated 5015 passes through University Circle. The former Elysium skating rink, later a used-car dealership, is in the background. *(Anthony Krisak photo)*

In 1948, CTS 5018 has just passed Lakeview Cemetery on Euclid Avenue near East 120th Street. *(Jim Spangler collection)*

The Hayden Avenue branch of the Euclid car line enjoyed a stretch of private right-of-way. Here car 5002 is inbound, nearing Windermere Station. *(Cleveland State University Michael Schwartz Library, Bruce Young Collection)*

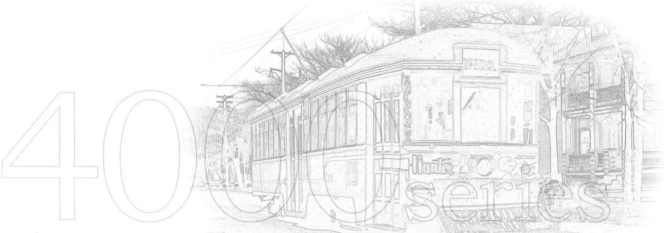

CLEVELAND RAILWAY'S 4000 SERIES PETER WITTS

At the same time that Cleveland Railway received its first articulated unit from G. C. Kuhlman, it also took possession of a single car unit, numbered 333. The car was built with the same amenities as 5000, and its interior space and external lines were similar, except that its center doors were positioned at the car's actual center whereas the "center" door on the front car of the articulated unit was placed farther towards the rear. Like 5000, car 333 also made its debut with split destination signs at front and center and three equally sized front windows. These features were changed (to single destination signs and a broader front window) on all production models. Car 333, renumbered as 4000, was retrofitted to this modified look.

Altogether, Cleveland Railway ordered 150 of these modern single units. The fleet, CR Type 32, were assigned numbers 4000-4149. After receiving the first unit in 1927, the Railway took delivery of the remainder of the fleet between September 1928

and May 1930. The cost of each car was $18,000.00. The 4000s were put into service on 10 of the busiest lines throughout the system, but the east side was serviced by 100 of the new cars to 50 that plied the rails of the west side.

A rebuilding program that began in 1939 gave all of the fleet new interior lighting, replacing the dome lights in the center aisle with bullet lighting above each seat. The cars were also given new interior paint jobs, and new rubber flooring added to passenger safety.

In 1939 Cleveland Railway also introduced a new exterior paint scheme to its fleet, the work of the nationally prominent industrial designer, Raymond Loewy. The Company's simple yellow and cream design was replaced by a more dynamic look, featuring a combination of dark green, grey, and white. This repainting began with car 4073, and then went on to encompass almost two thirds of the 4000 fleet. An increase in night-time accidents, however, soon convinced Company officials that the new paint scheme was too dark, and in 1941 it was replaced by a combination of an orange brown and cream, with brown striping. The first car to receive the brighter treatment was 4066. This new paint scheme was then applied to all the streetcar fleets, and it remained the choice until the end of streetcar service 13 years later.

The 4000s were the last active streetcars in Cleveland, continuing in service until the Madison Avenue line changed over to bus operation on January 24, 1954. On that day, the Cleveland *Press* sponsored a day of free final streetcar trips between downtown and West 65th Street. That day car 4142 was the very last streetcar to operate.

Only one car escaped the scrapping of the 4000 fleet that was carried out during 1953 and 1954. Car 4144 was bought by railfan Norman Muller and moved to South Lorain, Ohio. Unfortunately, community officials and neighbors objected to its presence, and Muller eventually succumbed to their pressure and scrapped the car.

In 1928, on Kuhlman Car Company tracks the first car of the 4000 series is ready for acceptance by the Cleveland Railway Company. Originally numbered 333, it will later become 4000.
(Cleveland State University Michael Schwartz Library, Gerald E. Brookins Collection)

The interior of CRC 4094 shows its comfortable transverse leather seating throughout the car and the domed ceiling lights along the center aisle. *(Jim Spangler collection)*

CRC 4073 shows the changes in the interior following a 1939 rebuilding of the fleet. The interior is brighter with new light-colored paint. Bullet lights above each seat have replaced the former globe fixtures along the center aisle. *(Cleveland State University Michael Schwartz Library, Gerald E. Brookins Collection)*

In 1939, Cleveland Railway began a livery overhaul for its streetcar fleet.
Here a 4000 series car is receiving the new look. *(Cleveland Railway photo)*

Parked at Harvard Yard, CRC 4149 and 4073 model two generations of paint. Car 4149 is in the original Railway yellow, and 4073 bears the new green, gray, and white. It was the first car to receive the modern paint job.
(Cleveland State University Michael Schwartz Library, Gerald E. Brookins Collection, Harry Christiansen photo)

In Broadway service, car 4130 stops at the railroad crossing on Miles Avenue at East 102nd Street. *(Bill Vigrass photo)*

The side-of-the-road reservation on Cedar Hill carried streetcars to and from suburban Cleveland Heights. The Cedar, Fairmount, and Mayfield car lines all used this trackage. Car 4053 is heading for downtown Cleveland in 1947.
(Cleveland State University Michael Schwartz Library, Bruce Young Collection)

Car 4033 rests in the Spring Garden wye in Lakewood, the western end of the Madison streetcar line.
(Cleveland State University Michael Schwartz Library, Gerald E. Brookins Collection, Harry Christiansen photo)

In April, 1951, CTS 4074 and 4122 emerge from the Detroit-Superior subway at
West Sixth Street and Superior Avenue.   *(Herb Harwood photo)*

CTS 4003, on the Detroit Avenue line, is at Rocky River Station on August 23, 1951.
Streetcars on Detroit only have two more days. *(Anthony Krisak photo)*

Decorated to mark the last day for streetcar operations in Cleveland, January 24, 1954, CTS 4138
is westbound on the subway level of the Detroit-Superior Bridge. (*Anthony Krisak photo*)

A sad scene for streetcar fans---CTS 4117 succumbs to the wrecking crew at Harvard Yard in 1954.
(*Jim Spangler photo*)

EPILOG

The Peter Witt car was invented in Cleveland, and during the city's streetcar days some 558 streetcars of the Witt design rumbled over the city's track network. The influence of the model transformed public transit across America. It is ironic, then, that no Cleveland Peter Witts have survived. Trolley museums around the country fortunately have Peter Witt model cars in their collections, but none from Cleveland. In their home city, the rail abandonment came too soon, before interest in historic preservation had sufficiently matured. Thank goodness, then, for the photographers who so thoroughly recorded a dynamic era in their city's transportation history. The authors salute them, particularly: Roy Bruce, Jim Buckley, Harry Christiansen, Herb Harwood, Anthony Krisak, Steve McGuire, Frank Novak, Bernard Polinak, Bill Scholes, Russ Schram, and Bill Vigrass.

ACKNOWLEDGMENTS

We would also like to express our appreciation to Bill Barrow and Lynn Duchez-Bycko of Cleveland State University Michael Schwartz Library's Special Collections for their dedicated work in preserving the rail history of Cleveland and for making it so readily available to patrons. We thank John Yasenosky, III, for once again making our work look good. And finally, we express our gratitude to Greg Deegan, Dan Cook, and Kathy Cook of Cleveland Landmarks Press for their unflagging support.

One Peter Witt car briefly escaped the scrap line. CTS 4144 was bought by Lorain County resident Norman Muller and became a stationary display on his property. A Cleveland Southwestern interurban fan, Muller painted the car in the interurban's green livery. The car was finally scrapped in 1962. *(Frank Novak photo)*